Operations Management
in a week

SEAN NAUGHTON

ghton

OF THE HODDER HEADLINE GROUP

Orders: please contact Bookpoint Ltd, 130 Milton Park, Abingdon, Oxon OX14 4SB.
Telephone: (44) 01235 827720, Fax: (44) 01235 400454. Lines are open from 9.00 -
6.00, Monday to Saturday, with a 24 hour message answering service.
Email address: orders@bookpoint.co.uk

British Library Cataloguing in Publication Data
A catalogue record for this title is available from The British Library

ISBN 0 340 849665

First published 1999
Impression number   10 9 8 7 6 5 4 3 2 1
Year   2007 2006 2005 2004 2003 2002

Typeset by SX Composing DTP, Rayleigh, Essex
Printed in Great Britain for Hodder & Stoughton Educational, a division of
Hodder Headline Plc, 338 Euston Road, London NW1 3BH by
Cox & Wyman Ltd, Reading, Berkshire.

C O N T E N T S

Just before midnight on 14 April 1912, more than 1500 people tragically lost their lives on board *The Titanic*. The investigation that followed discovered the ship was travelling too quickly in dangerous waters; there were too few lifeboats for passengers and crew; and the nearest vessel within radio contact knew nothing about the incident, as the radio operator was asleep.

This tragedy should have been a warning to the world, and to some extent, lessons were learnt. History, however, documents many organisations that have not realised they operate in a similar way to that infamous ship.

Managing operations is a vital part of every organisation. Although it is not always recognised as such, Operations Management involves everyone from the managing director to the lowest paid worker. Those organisations not seriously considering Operations Management codes are working along the *Titanic Management Principle*:

Under this principle, the organisation cruises along until a serious problem arises – the proverbial iceberg! In response, managers seal the nearest partition with the loss of a department. This change is disturbing, but the organisation continues its voyage. When the next unavoidable *iceberg* is hit, managers implement the same emergency procedure.

There is logic to this pattern. After all, if there is a hole, why not plug it?

The ultimate dilemma arrives when there are no more doors to shut. Everything within the organisation that could have been ignored *has been* ignored. At this dire

> moment, an imposing iceberg rips through several
> sections of the organisation. The few available lifeboats
> are filled. For anyone remaining, the only way is down,
> just as it was on 14 April 1912.

The *Titanic Management Principle*, though polar opposite to
our goals, is a powerful teacher from whom we can learn and
benefit – avoiding the mistakes made by organisations that
have perished in its path.

By reading this book, you will see how Operations
Management is the foundation of all successful organisations.
Effective Operations Managers are voracious and unbound in
their search of excellence. Whilst some naturally strive for
perfection, others happily work with tried and tested
methods, tools and techniques.

By exploring the phenominal benefits these methods and
techniques hold, you will be left contemplating how *you* can
put them to good use to make your own organisation truly
world class.

We shall look at one step each day of the week.

Sunday	What is Operations Management?
Monday	Volume versus variety
Tuesday	Managing quality
Wednesday	Project planning and control
Thursday	Managing people
Friday	Operations Management and computers
Saturday	The strategic challenge facing Operations Management

What is Operations Management?

Today we will consider the fundamentals of Operations Management, and will go some way to answering the question: *what is Operations Management?*

Sunday – turn of events

- The Operations Management Concept
- Why study Operations Management in organisations?
- What Operations Managers do
- Why did Operations Management evolve?
- Operations Management and change

The Operations Management concept

Many people regard *Operations Management* to be a mysterious process that has no meaning to them because they do not work in a manufacturing environment. This is far from the truth – *everyone*, no matter what job they hold, is affected by Operations Management.

So, what exactly is it?

Operations Management is the set of activities creating goods or services through transforming inputs into outputs.

Inputs	Outputs
• Land	• Products
• Labour	• Services
• Capital	• Profits
• Entrepreneurship	• Employment
• Equipment	• Skills . . .
• Skills	
• Time	
• Training . . .	

We can represent this *input/output* concept diagrammatically:

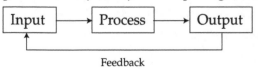

Feedback

We have integrated *feedback* into the model. This is the communication link between the output and any future input into the system. It can be seen as a quality checking operation which allows us to take corrective action. Whilst this may seem an oddity, we can illustrate the point through the use of the simple example of preparing boiled eggs.

We make use of inputs in the form of eggs, water, a pan and gas. The water and raw eggs are placed in the pan and heated. The chef knows that the eggs must be in the boiling water for at least five minutes before they will be ready. Even with this in mind, continuous checks are made to ensure the eggs are cooked correctly. When the chef is satisfied that the eggs are ready they are removed from the boiling water – and eaten. Again, we can show this diagrammatically:

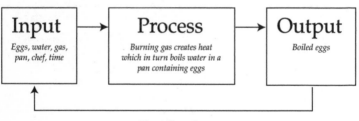

Feedback

The *feedback* line is representative of the chef checking the pan of eggs to make sure the water never boils over or the pan boils dry, and to see if the eggs are cooked. Feedback is something we use all the time – often without realising it. Whenever we write letters we read them before sending, whilst talking to someone we watch their expressions to make sure they understand us. These are just a few examples of feedback.

Why study Operations Management in organisations?

Operations Management is one of the three major aspects of every organisation. The other two are *marketing* and *finance*. Whilst we may perceive the activities of service and manufacturing organisations to be different, they are in fact very similar. One might produce tangible goods such as televisions, and the other produces services such as banking – but the three main functions they perform are similar. We can see this in the following charts:

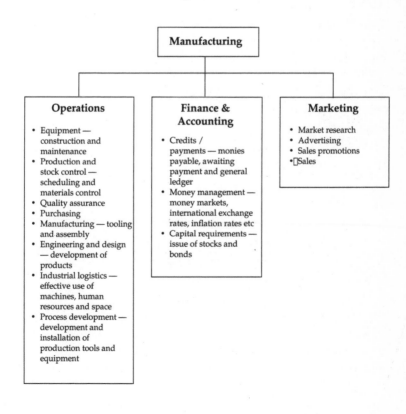

Manufacturing

Operations
- Equipment — construction and maintenance
- Production and stock control — scheduling and materials control
- Quality assurance
- Purchasing
- Manufacturing — tooling and assembly
- Engineering and design — development of products
- Industrial logistics — effective use of machines, human resources and space
- Process development — development and installation of production tools and equipment

Finance & Accounting
- Credits / payments — monies payable, awaiting payment and general ledger
- Money management — money markets, international exchange rates, inflation rates etc
- Capital requirements — issue of stocks and bonds

Marketing
- Market research
- Advertising
- Sales promotions
- Sales

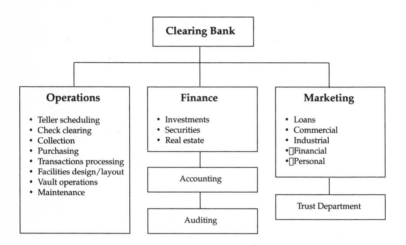

By studying Operations Management we gain a better understanding of how all organisations operate. Not only does this help us do our jobs more effectively, but it *should* help for our next job application – it makes little difference whether the organisation manufactures sweets or helicopters, or deals with insurance claims – the Operations Management functions will be closely related.

Operations Management makes us:

- become aware of how people organise themselves for productive enterprise
- see how goods and services are produced
- understand where production costs in organisations exist – we can then target these areas for improvement

What Operations Managers do

Not every Operations Manager necessarily carries the *Operations Management* title. It would be fair to argue that we are all Operations Managers to some degree as we plan our work around certain criteria:

Operations Management Planning Criteria

- **Control** – create and maintain a positive flow of work, utilising all resources and facilities available
- **Lead** – develop and cascade the organisation strategy or mission statement to staff, leading by example
- **Organise** – resources, facilities and employees to ensure the effective production of goods or services
- **Plan** – balance customer, employee and organisational requirements

- **Staff** – monitor and maintain staffing levels, skills, expectations and motivation, in order to fulfil organisational requirements
- **Performance measures** – develop methods for measuring performance, and consider efficiency vs effectiveness

Why did Operations Management evolve?

Operations Management is a relatively new concept, dating back to 1776 with Adam Smith's *Division of Labour* inspiration. From a practical business perspective, Henry Ford is credited as being the first to turn the Operations Management philosophy to his financial advantage when he mass-produced the Model T.

By today's standards, the Ford production facilities of 1913 are antiquated, particularly as robots were noticeable by their absence. Instead, Ford made use of people. He broke down and simplified the task of car manufacture, giving individuals one job to do all day long. He assumed that by doing this, the individuals would become experts at their jobs, and find means to improve the ways in which they worked. Whilst his assumption was effective for some time, he failed to realise that he was in fact dealing with *people* – individuals with feelings – a fact he was eventually forced to accept.

Operations Management was plunged into the position of *having* to evolve to make best use of resources. Whilst Ford's scientific approach failed to work in the long term, there were a number of Operations Managers and psychologists waiting in the wings to offer new inspiration, as we can see in the following Operations Management heritage table:

Division of Labour – Adam Smith	1776
Standardised Parts – Whitney	1800
Division of Labour – Charles Babbage	1852
Scientific Management – Taylor	1881
Co-ordinated Assembly Line – Ford/Sorenson/Avery	1913
Gantt Charts – Gantt	1916
Motion Study – Frank & Lillian Gilbreth	1922
Quality Control – Shewhart	1924
Computer – Atanasoff	1938
Quality Control – Deming	1950
Critical Path Method / PERT – DuPont	1957
Material Requirements Planning (MRP) – Orlicky	1960
Computer Aided Design	1970
Flexible Manufacturing Systems	1973
Baldridge Quality	1980
Computer Integrated Manufacture	1990
Internet	1995

It is widely recognised that manufacturing in the UK began lagging behind competing nations after World War II. This was partly due to complacency and bad planning on our behalf – after all, we had won the war and were the best there was. Everything we could make sold, so why should we have reinvested back into our own organisations?

The answer started to become apparent in the 1960s when competitor organisations from Europe and Japan began to conquer our markets. They began by copying *our* products and gradually improved their own product quality. Within a relatively short period, world markets that had once been British dominated, were no longer accessible to many western organisations.

Operations Management and change

It makes no difference whether an Operations Manager works in the service or production sectors, the individual in question will very often be seen as a *change agent*. In truth, a good Operations Manager will be analysing situations and making changes constantly. Ideally, he or she will be expecting, challenging and developing others to do the same. The name of the game here is *improvement*.

It would appear that the Japanese are world champions at

making improvements. Their word Kaizen has been widely adopted as a standard of excellence for change and improvement. Kaizen comes from the words *Kai* meaning *change* and Zen meaning *good*. Through Kaizen, workplace improvements are made through small and often systematic steps. Such changes must be driven by internal and external customers.

Most people tend to see customers as being the people or organisations that buy goods and services from us. The Kaizen model forces us to recognise customers as anyone that is part of the *input-process-output* chain that passes finished or part-finished work on to someone else. For most of us therefore, this means that our colleagues are our customers and it is up to us to satisfy their needs. This is often very difficult. To meet requirements we may be forced to ask one another what our internal customers expect of us. If we fail to collect and collate this information, our customers' needs are unlikely to be met successfully.

To make Kaizen truly effective, an organisation must involve everyone through systematic and open communications. Kaizen sees people as an organisation's most important asset, and this makes teamwork, openness and information sharing vitally important. Without effective channels of communication and a co-operative workforce, Kaizen is effectively made redundant.

Kaizen Considers:

- Customer satisfaction
- Total quality (with zero defects)
- JIT (Just In Time production)
- Cross-functional management
- Policy development
- Total productive maintenance
- Good housekeeping
- The elimination of anything *not* adding value
- Continuous improvement cycles
- Quality circles
- Visual management

Over the next six days we will work through the practical aspects of Operations Management in some detail. We continue tomorrow by looking at the *volume* versus *variety* debate.

Summary

We have spent Sunday examining the notion of Operations Management. In so doing we have looked at:

- The Operations Management concept
- Inputs, outputs, processes and feedback
- The similarities for Operations Management between goods and services
- The planning criteria for Operations Management
- The evolvement of Operations Management
- The need for *change* in Operations Management

Volume versus variety

Following Sunday's work, we now know what Operations Management is all about. Today we will look at some of the most common concepts associated with efficiently turning inputs into outputs:

Monday – turn of events

- The Just In Case concept (JIC)
- The Just In Time concept (JIT)
- Volume versus variety
- Capacity management
- The importance of layout
- Material Requirements Planning (MRP)
- Manufacturing Resources Planning (MRP II)

The Just In Case concept – JIC

Ideally, when a customer requires one of our products or services, we should supply it there and then. If we fail to make this instant provision then we lose the sale to a competitor. Worse still, there is a good chance that the customer will be lost forever to our competitor.

Traditionally, Western organisations have found that the simplest way to fulfil this expectation has been to hold stocks of the finished goods *just in case* customers need them. An everyday example of this can be seen in a supermarket – they hold goods on shelves in case customers want to buy them. As this is not always the case, there is a reasonable amount of waste that is either sold off at a reduced rate at the end of the day or else thrown away. Any business not achieving the right balance of goods that people want is likely to lose a lot of money with the possibility of bankruptcy just around the corner.

To sell finished goods or services in this way, the producing organisations must be one step ahead of the game – they need stocks of raw materials to make them in the first place.

One line of thought that ensures manufacturing *inputs* are ready for use as and when they are required is JIC (Just In Case). Here the producer of the goods or services holds stocks of resources so they are readily available for whenever production starts.

In Western manufacturing environments, the JIC concept has been taken to extremes when raw materials and other *inputs* have been ordered in bulk and kept in stock. This benefits the organisation by ensuring there are no *stock-outs* – input materials are always available when required.

In some respects this makes financial sense – it is extremely costly to halt production (and very annoying when it is due to lack of raw materials) – and suppliers are generally willing to offer discounts when purchasing materials in bulk.

Storing raw materials does require space which is obviously expensive. It also means that working capital is tied up in stock. This is again expensive – either because the capital has to be borrowed (with interest rates levied) or because it is money that could be invested to show a better return elsewhere in the business.

The Just In Time concept – JIT

In the 1970s, the Japanese began to make serious inroads into markets the West had always dominated. There were many reasons for this seemingly sudden turn of events, but one was related to the *Just In Case* philosophy. While western organisations were paying cripplingly high interest rates for holding stocks of raw materials, the Japanese were seemingly holding no stock at all. Japanese organisations were taking stocks of raw materials from suppliers only when they were

needed. In reality this could mean they were taking ownership of parts for a car as little as twenty minutes before they were assembled to the vehicle. The Just In Case philosophy long cherished by the West had been superceded by one based upon a zero stock concept: the Just In Time theory was on the move.

The JIT philosophy is more sophisticated than it might at first appear. Underneath this simple concept lies an effective and powerful management tool.

Just In Time has the intentions of:

- Meeting demand instantly
- Eliminating in-house stocks
- Eliminating waste
- Eliminating unimportant activities
- Eliminating poor suppliers
- Striving for perfect quality goods and services
- Highlighting potential problems before they strike!

Whilst many people consider the idea of eliminating stock pointless, if not dangerous (what if a supplier is late with a delivery?), consider the following diagrams:

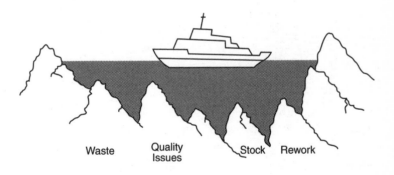

Waste   Quality Issues   Stock   Rework

Here, the inventory levels (represented by the sea level) are high enough for the ship to sail wherever it wishes – totally unaware of any problems that may exist beneath it. This may seem ideal, but sooner or later the problems will surface – possibly when it is too late.

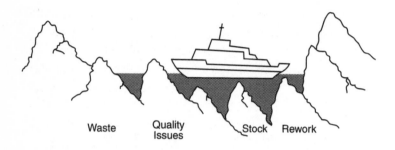

Waste   Quality Issues   Stock   Rework

In this second diagram, the inventory levels are lowered and problems exposed. If these problems are solved, the inventory can be further reduced and problems that would have been tolerated in the past will surface, so they too can be tackled.

This example appears to be dedicated to manufacturing operations, but that is not the case. Service organisations, like hospitals, make effective use of the JIT philosophy when dealing with stocks such as bandages and high use materials.

More importantly, on an individual basis we can all make use of the JIT concept. Consider the ideal desk at work – it is always empty! The moment any work is placed on it, the occupant ensures it is done. At the same time, consider a desk holding piles of work. How does the occupant know how long it will take to complete? Can accuracy be guaranteed if different projects are being worked on simultaneously? How much of it is for the bin? Questions like these highlight the fact that eliminating stock and clutter from the workplace make it easier to effectively and efficiently tackle the job in hand.

Volume versus variety

As an Operations Manager, possibly the most fundamental issue to be tackled even before JIC or JIT are considered relates to the *volume/variety* contingent. Are we dealing with high or low volume sales from our goods and services? If we are dealing with a high volume turnover, as in the case of a fast food hamburger restaurant, there is little scope to offer clients a wide variety of goods. If on the other hand we are dealing with a low volume turnover, as in the case of a prestigious restaurant, the chef can more or less alter the menu according to the requirements of customers, the variety here being virtually limitless.

There are of course variations in any operation, and the more competition there is in a given market, the more suppliers try to give their customers exactly what they want. For instance, exclusive restaurants often introduce *happy hours* to tempt customers away from less expensive but competing establishments, whilst the hamburger bar may advertise the fact that customers can have their burgers cooked *as they like them* and not in the standard way.

The differences between such establishments is, on the surface, minimal – after all, they both supply food to satisfy customers' hunger. The true differences are in their responsiveness to certain criteria:

Volume versus variety performance criteria

	Hamburger Bar	Exclusive Restaurant
Quality	Food looks the same as in adverts as well as tasting good. Clean eating area.	Food tastes exceptional and is well presented on individual plates. Ambience is important to the overall enjoyment of the food.
Speed	Instantly available.	Less important.
Flexibility	Little scope for flexibility by the nature of the product. A hamburger is always just a hamburger!	Large scope for the customer's culinary requirements to be met by the skilled and dedicated chef.
Dependability	Customers expect such products to be available as and when they want them – wherever they are!	Expectations are based upon receiving something *special* on each visit.
Cost	Goods are sensitive to pricing – if similar goods can be bought cheaply elsewhere, the customer will take the cheaper option.	The experience tends to be more important than the cost.

Capacity management

Whether an organisation sells goods or services, it is vitally important to know what the *capacity* or *maximum output* is. It is impossible to know exactly what this figure is, but accuracy helps – the bigger the margin or error, the bigger the chance of failure!

For example, think about an organisation that sells consultancy services. There is no point in the outfit employing 25 industrial consultants if there is only a market need at any one time for 15! Similarly, there is no point in employing ten consultants as market demand is exceeding supply and opportunities are being lost. If this were the case, other firms would quickly realise the error and clinch the market as their own.

Whilst these examples have been based upon service organisations, the arguments are very similar for a manufacturing operation – there is little point in renting a building big enough to house a car plant if only five people are to be employed there. This is excess capacity.

AND I TOLD YOU WE CAN MAKE TWO MILLION...

So how do organisations and operations managers budget for capacity?

Whenever anyone starts a new venture, there ought to be some consideration as to the capacity being dealt with – after all, what is the minimum *output* the organisation can operate at to make a profit?

As an example, consider a hotel with 50 fifty rooms. When unoccupied, each room costs £10 a night to run (the fixed costs). When occupied, each room costs an extra £5 a night (variable costs for laundry and housekeeping). Assuming full occupancy, the total fixed costs are £500 (50 × £10) a night, and the total variable costs are £250 (50 × £5) a night. If the hotel charges guests £30 per room a night, total revenue is £1500 (50 × £30). Nightly profit is therefore £750 [£1500 – (£500 + £250)] a night.

If occupancy levels fall to 40%, the total costs and the total revenue are £600 each. Profit is therefore nil. This is the *break even point* for the hotel – occupancy must therefore be greater than 40% to make a profit. We can see this graphically:

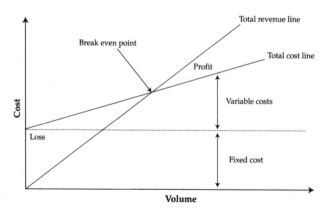

Interpreting the graph:

Fixed costs	Costs incurred even without units being produced e.g. heating
Variable costs	Costs that vary with the volume of units produced
Total cost line	The sum of all costs over a given period
Total revenue line	The sum of all income over a given period
Break even point	The point in time when costs = revenue. Neither profit nor loss is made at this point

So with this model in mind, organisations can calculate the capacity they require and volume of units that **must** be sold, and at what price, so as to break even and ultimately make a profit.

The importance of layout

Layout is particularly important to operations management – get it right and the long-run efficiency of operations is much improved. Get it wrong and life becomes more difficult. Consider again the example at one's desk. Most people will agree that they are most effective when the layout of their desk is uncluttered and they can concentrate solely on one task – photographs and toys on the desk do not help either! From an organisation's point of view, effective layout assists with regard to capacity, processes, flexibility, cost and quality of working life.

An effective layout can achieve:

- Better use of space, equipment and personnel
- Improved flow of information, components and personnel
- Enhanced availability for the customer
- Safer working conditions and higher employee morale

In order to realise such benefits from an effective layout, organisations must consider factors, such as the arrangement of desks, equipment and machines, to ensure the highest levels of operation and efficiency between sections.

There are six *types* of layout that can be employed to bring about the required outcome for organisations:

Layout type	Use
Fixed position	For large projects such as building work
Process-oriented	For low volume, highly diversified products
Office	Location of personnel, offices and equipment to ensure the free flow of information
Retail/service	Use of shelf space to entice customers to buy more goods!

| Product-oriented | Makes best use of equipment and people in continuous production |
| Warehouse | Considers the options between handling materials and the space available |

Material Requirements Planning – MRP

We have so far considered eliminating stock, the variety of products or services we offer, economic production goals and layout. Whilst each of these factors is vitally important in its own right, we need ideally to integrate them together to be truly effective in our output.

Whilst organisations realise that holding stock is not ideal, from a practical point at least, stock has to be held – it is too risky not to hold some raw materials . The real question is how much should be stored for each product or service offered? MRP was devised to help solve the issue.

With MRP, organisations break down the products or services they sell into their component parts. Based upon *historical* sales data, a prediction is made as to how many of these parts will be required over the coming period, and components are ordered accordingly. This simple concept is complicated by including such factors as the effects of demand brought about by the forthcoming season and its likely weather, population trends and world economic factors. With such statistics included, the process does as its name implies – it *plans the materials that will be required*. Whilst it can be done by hand, MRP systems really require computers due to the vast number of calculations that have to be performed. A tool such as MRP is of course just as useful in a restaurant or hospital as an ordering system, as it is in a manufacturing environment.

Benefits of MRP:

- Improved customer service and satisfaction
- Improved use of equipment and personnel
- Improved planning and control of stocks
- Improved response to market variations
- Reduced stock levels

Whilst MRP offers a number of benefits, it does carry less welcome baggage too – it requires a huge investment in terms of money and time. It also requires computer-loving people to make it work. Others dislike the change it brings.

Manufacturing Resources Planning – MRP II

MRP II came about as an extension to MRP – it incorporates the concepts dealt with so far regarding materials, but goes on to examine the effects on future demand for an organisation's financial position, people and equipment. Ultimately – it should balance all factors of output so that supplies and customer demand are perfectly matched.

In truth, none of the concepts dealt with today work perfectly. They generally require intervention by someone with knowledge, experience – and a hunch!

Summary

We have spent Monday investigating a number of techniques that can be employed for effectively turning inputs into outputs. In doing so we have considered:

- The case for holding stocks of components
- The case for eliminating stock
- Balancing volume and variety
- Using costing methods to estimate volume
- Options available regarding layout
- Forecasting models (MRP and MRP II)

Managing quality

We have so far considered how to turn inputs into outputs, and have assumed that outputs are always perfect. As this is not the case, we need to address the matter of *quality*:

> *Tuesday – turn of events*
>
> * The quality concept
> * Total Quality Management (TQM)
> * Business Process Reengineering (BPR)
> * British standards and international standards
> * Statistical Process Control (SPC)
> * Quality awards

The quality concept

In the past *quality* was seen as a luxury – it was something one paid extra for. Examples are plentiful but one of the most common is that of a car – the basic concept of a car is that it is a vehicle that transports people from one place to another. Why then do people purchase different makes and models of cars? Surely all cars do the same job whether they cost £8,000 or £80,000?

In today's markets, quality is no longer a luxury. For those organisations wishing to succeed it is a necessity that they build quality into all products and services. Any organisation that sells products or services of poor quality will simply fail to make sales and will not survive in tomorrow's world.

Odd as it seems, *cost* is no longer the major factor of *quality*.

Thinking back to the example of the cars again, we can ask the question as to which is the better quality vehicle – the car for £8,000 or the one for £80,000? The answer should be *they are both of equal quality*. The car costing £80,000 should be more luxurious and may offer a better ride, but the build quality of both the cars and their components ought to be the same. This has not always been the case though.

At the end of World War II, UK companies that had managed to survive were in a strong and enviable position. As there was such high demand for all products and services, they could sell whatever they could produce, no matter how good or bad they were. By today's standards it seems ludicrous to think that customers made life even easier for the producers by expecting things to go wrong with the products they bought. The times of guarantees and legal requirements had not yet arrived.

During this time of western organisation dominance, the Japanese were rebuilding their economic infrastructure and began to work at selling their products to the rest of the world. At first the buying public viewed the Japanese products suspiciously. This was hardly surprising as the Japanese organisations often built little more than poor quality copies of western goods.

It wasn't until the 1950s that the importance of *quality* began to become more meaningful in the eyes of the purchaser. This was largely due to the promotion of the quality concept for goods and services by the gurus Deming and Juran. Their messages were largely ignored in the West – after all, why change a winning formula? The Japanese however realised that this was their opportunity and seized it in their bid for competitive advantage. They listened carefully to Deming and Juran's messages and implemented them.

When western organisations finally began to consider quality issues, they made use of them as *inspection tools* at the end of production runs. The Japanese on the other hand were working with quality as a method of *prevention – making the product right first time and every time*. Whilst both sides were now implementing *quality*, the Japanese benefited most. This was down to *cost*. By producing goods and services *right first time*, there was no need for inspection, rejection and rework. Many people correctly assume the Western processes were extensive, but few would guess that their elimination could realistically have saved an organisation 25% of its sales revenue.

Since the start of the quality revolution, a number of other gurus have built upon Deming's original concept and added their own ideas to quality theory:

Quality gurus	Their quality concepts
Deming	Management Philosophy
Juran	Planning, Quality Costs
Feigenbaum	Total Quality Control
Ishikawa	Simple Tools, Quality Circles, Company-wide Quality
Taguchi	Minimum Prototyping
Shigeo Shingo	Poka-Yoke/Zero Defects
Crosby	Awareness, Zero Defects, Right First Time
Peters	Customer Orientation
Moller	Personal Quality
Oakland	TQM

SO QUALITY ISN'T QUITE UP TO WHERE WE EXPECTED IT TO BE THEN?

Total Quality Management – TQM

From time to time, it is not unusual to stop and ask yourself the question "what is *quality*?" Quality means different things to different people. Some people argue that to them, a quality car is one with the right badge on the front. Others argue a quality car is one that does not break down between services.

Total Quality Management offers a standard interpretation for its role in the world of quality.

Total means that every member of an organisation is concerned with the product or service being sold to the consumer.

Quality is more difficult to define. Laws throughout the world refer to quality products as those that are *fit for purpose*. Alternatively, we see a quality good or service as one that *conforms to or exceeds our requirements*.

Management is the activity that makes the entire process work. It makes use of personnel, capital and any other resources available.

To ensure an organisation sustains competitive advantage and meets its financial targets, TQM focuses primarily on:

- **Customers** – what do they specifically want?

- **Processes** – are they efficient and effective?

- **Workforce empowerment** – can individuals make decisions for themselves?

- **Continuous improvement** – is the workforce aware they *can* make improvements to the ways in which they perform their jobs?

- **Leadership** – often requiring training

- **Measurement** – of outputs, profits and effectiveness.

Whilst TQM is obviously concerned with quality, we can see from the *focus* list above that it strives for quality by tackling all the issues that *could potentially* create poor quality goods or services. If there are no excuses for poor output then it simply cannot exist!

The reasons for implementing the Total Quality Management tool are:

- Survival

- Elimination of waste

- To compete with the world-wide increase in competition

- To empower employees

- A *marketing* tool – customers now take more interest in how goods and services are produced

The benefits of Total Quality Management:

- Elimination of waste

- Employee empowerment leading to self managed teams

- Enhanced products and services

- Increase in competitive advantage

- Increase in market share

- Increase in productivity

- Increase in profits

- Motivated workforce

Business Process Reengineering – BPR

The notion of Business Process Reegineering being incorporated into the subject of *quality* may seem unusual, but the quality world has much to gain from it.

BPR is concerned with radically re-thinking and re-designing processes to bring about improvements in performance. This means we may have to scrap old processes – probably the familiar and easy ones we have been working with for many years – and start again with a clean sheet of paper.

A CLEAN SHEET OF PAPER... YES...HAHAHA FOR A MOMENT THERE I THOUGHT YOU ASKED ME TO DEVISE NEW PROCESSES!

An obvious question here is why? Can your organisation answer the following questions?

- Is the organisation working perfectly?

- Is there room for improvement?

- Each time an improvement is made, is it merely tacked on to the end of the present process?

- Does this make it more difficult to work?

- If so then why not scrap the old method with its complicated ways and begin again – afresh?

The underlying thought behind BPR is that operations should be organised around the processes that add value to goods and services for the customer. Operations should not be organised around *what we can do*.

The principles of BPR are:

- Redesigning processes around what the product or service requires rather than having the product or service evolving around the processes

- By redesigning processes there will be a dramatic increase in performance

- Making employees see the results of their outputs – possibly through job rotation

- Make people responsible for making decisions for the work they do

With these points in mind, it is not unfair to argue that BPR is very similar to TQM. The difference is that TQM is concerned with an entire organisation, while BPR is concerned with possibly just one individual process within an organisation.

British and international standards

In a bid to secure international quality recognition between organisations, a set of internationally recognised standards has been devised. ISO 9000 provides a framework for quality assurance throughout the world. Oddly, this does not mean it is recognised in every country. Some nations insist upon dealing only with organisations that hold their own national ISO equivalent standard. Examples of ISO equivalents are: the UK BS5750, the Australian AS3900.

The purpose of ISO 9000 and its *nationalised cousins* is to guarantee to anyone buying products or sevices that their build quality meets requirements. This is achieved by outlining standards, procedures and features of the management system controlling the business.

QUALITY ASSURED

The ISO 9000 framework makes use of five clearly defined areas:

> - **ISO 9000** – "quality management and quality assurance standards and guidelines for selection and use."
>
> - **ISO 9001** – "quality systems model for quality assurance in design/development, production, installation and servicing."
>
> - **ISO 9002** – "quality systems model for quality assurance in production and installation."
>
> - **ISO 9003** – "quality systems model for quality assurance in final inspection and test."
>
> - **ISO 9004** – "quality management and quality system elements: guidelines."

To qualify for ISO status an organisation must have its quality standards and procedures assessed by a third party. Once ISO standing is achieved, the standards and procedures are audited on a regular basis to guarantee their use and maintenance.

ISO 9000 accreditation holds a number of benefits:

- The framework supplies a disciplined approach to work
- When writing and developing ISO procedures, organisations identify unnecessary areas of work and eliminate them – thus saving money
- It can help to reduce waste, mistakes, customer complaints and costs
- Holding ISO status is a strong marketing tool for an organisation

The disadvantages of ISO 9000 are:

- The five parts to ISO 9000 look similar – organisations find it difficult to decide which section to apply for
- ISO procedures *can* make work regimented and bureaucratic
- ISO guidelines tend to be geared towards production rather than service based organisations
- ISO guidelines tend not to refer to quality issues that organisations may already be committed to
- Obtaining and maintaining ISO status is time consuming and costly for all organisations

Statistical Process Control – SPC

As with so many other areas of business, some parts of the quality world makes use of statistics. SPC was developed as a means of examining products and services during their creation. If a problem occurs during this time, the process can be stopped and corrective action taken. SPC offers organisations a further important additional benefit – it highlights processes that appear to be going wrong or out of control and *could* produce faulty goods or services in the future.

In a perfect world, everything conforms exactly to its specification, but in reality this rarely happens. As long as goods and services conform within acceptable tolerances then everyone is happy. When working with SPC, these tolerances are borne in mind. Products or services are examined at different stages in the production process to see how closely they perform to specifications. Their details are noted on a graph that will end up looking like the one below with an upper and lower tolerance limit:

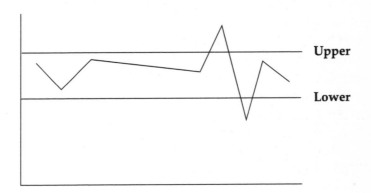

Provided the measurements fall in line with the tolerance limits, the process continues. If a measurement exceeds one of the limits then the process is halted and corrective action taken.

When creating SPC control charts it is important to ensure they are always drawn in a similar way so that new data can quickly and easily be compared to old.

Quality awards

To raise the national status of *quality*, many countries have devised their own national quality awards. Possibly the best known is the USA's Malcolm Baldridge Award. Not to be left behind, the European Quality Award (EQA) was introduced throughout Europe in 1992.

In 1958, fourteen companies throughout the Western Europe formed the European Foundation for Quality Management (EFQM) with the intention of recognising achievements in quality. It was the EFQM that established the European Quality Award (EQA). This prestigious honour goes to the most successful user of the TQM philosophy in Western Europe. To win the award, organisations must show that they use TQM to fulfil the expectations of customers, employees and society, as well as being models of excellence for other oganisations.

The major difference between the EQA and quality *enabling* standards is that the EQA is concerned with what a company has achieved and is achieving – enablers are interested in how results are being achieved.

The nine key areas the EQA is concerned with are:

1 Leadership
2 Policy and strategy
3 People management
4 Resources
5 Processes
6 Customer satisfaction
7 People satisfaction
8 Perception
9 Achievement

Summary

We have spent today in investigating the *quality* tools available to the Operations Manager. In so doing we have looked at:

- The quality concept and why it is necessary for customers today
- The use of TQM to improve quality throughout an entire organisation using the *clean sheet* approach
- The BPR tool and its benefits for operating improvements on a small scale, i.e. not organisation-wide
- The structures, benefits and downfalls of quality standards
- The measurement of quality using SPC
- The prestigious quality awards businesses can win

Project planning and control

Whilst still concerned with turning inputs into outputs, today we turn our attention today to Project Management.

Wednesday – turn of events

- Linking project management with operations management
- Project environment
- Project definition
- Project planning
- Project implementation
- Project control

Linking project management with operations management

Introducing project management in line with Operations Management may seem contrary, but many projects are run within Operations Management environments.

Project are usually, but not always, concerned with complicated and often large-scale activities. No matter what their size, all projects have defined starting and finishing dates – and a pre-determined end condition of course!

Examples of projects over recent years are:

- Construction of the Channel Tunnel
- Design and construction of Disneyland Paris
- Building the Millennium Dome

- Arranging and running a birthday party
- Running an Institute of Management conference
- Making a cup of tea!

Whilst they may seem radically different, the above examples of projects have many common elements:

- An objective
- A degree of complexity
- Each is a one-off
- A degree of uncertainty
- They are short-term
- Each has a finite life cycle

ANOTHER STAIR, ANOTHER PROJECT...

This does not mean that running projects is necessarily difficult. All projects require a degree of planning (no matter what their size) and this in turn requires forward thinking by

the project manager. But no matter how well a project is
planned, there are bound to be problems.

Successful projects tend to portray the following aspects:

- Explicit goals
- A skilled and knowledgeable project manager
- Senior management support
- Effective project team
- Adequate resources
- Effective means of communication
- Feedback mechanisms
- Close liaison with clients

*All projects must go through the following five stages if they are to
be successful:*

Stage 1	Project environment
Stage 2	Project definition
Stage 3	Project planning
Stage 4	Implementation
Stage 5	Project control

With the exception of *implementation* (physically running the
project), we shall look at each of them briefly in turn and later
put them into context using an example:

Project environment
Before people become involved in a project, they must be aware
of the environment in which it will operate. They will need to
know and understand factors such as location; who the

customers are and their individual expectations; end user requirements; and the resources that are available. In reality the list can be far more extensive and complicated than the previous simple outline might suggest because a true project environment is unique to each project and cannot be highlighted in a few lines. Nevertheless, the principles still stand.

Project definition

Running projects requires clarity. Everyone involved must know precisely what tasks they are to perform and when. Prior to issuing the workforce with such details, the project manager must clarify what objectives and range the project will have. These help to focus the project team on specific goals. Extra details may also be added including specified deadlines, any budgets and costs involved, and factors such as quality standards that must be met.

Project planning

If we don't plan, we don't know when we are getting things
right or wrong until it's too late. Lack of planning in projects
can result in expensive errors being made, particularly when
there are millions and possibly billions of pounds at stake.
Effective project planning will look at costing, non-financial
resources, work allocation and possible changes that may
have to be incorporated later on.

Project control

By their very nature, projects are relatively short lived and
require control – without it they overrun from a time and
cost perspective. In the worst case scenario, some projects
could even be left incomplete.

Project control incorporates scheduling, estimating, cost
control and material control.

These four work areas aim to achieve the following:

- **Scheduling** – design and develop timetables that
  highlight times at which different aspects of the
  project can be started and when they must be
  completed
- **Estimating** – predict volumes of materials, numbers
  of employees and costs that will be associated with a
  specific project
- **Cost control** – calculate ongoing costs associated
  with a particular project, and ensure expenditure is in
  line with estimates

- **Material control** – issue orders for materials and track their whereabouts and usage throughout the life of the project. Ideally, materials are delivered only when needed (thus cutting costs) – on a JIT basis

Having outlined the stages involved in project management, we can consider a simple example and contextualise it – making a cup of tea!

ANOTHER TEA HARRY?

THANKS REG, BUT DON'T WORRY ABOUT THE MILK RESOURCE AT STAGE 3

Stage 1 – Project environment

- User: me
- Suppliers: supermarket for tea, milk, sugar and kettle
- Electricity company
- Water company

Stage 2 – Project definition

Objective: to make a cup of tea
Scope: making use of a household electric kettle, equipment to keep materials fresh
Intention: by bringing together all fresh materials and equipment at the appropriate time

Stage 3 – Project planning

How many resources are required?
- 1 cup
- 1 tea bag
- milk
- water
- time

Stage 4 – Project control

Largely controlled by previous expectations as to how a cup of tea should be made.

Critical Path Analysis – CPA

Probably the most commonly used tool in the project manager's arsenal is Critical Path Analysis. It provides the means to manage any project, and bring about its completion in the shortest possible time and the most economical way.

CPA breaks a job down into its component tasks, sequencing and allocating completion times for each of them. This sequence is drawn up as a network that highlights the critical tasks that could delay the project as a whole. This string of critical tasks is known as the *critical path*.

Building on the last example of making a cup of tea, we will

show how CPA works. The first task is to break the job down
into its component chores. Furthermore, we will state the
order the tasks have to be performed in, and a duration in
seconds for each task. This will allow us to calculate finishing
times towards the end of the exercise.

*For the sake of example, we will keep it simple and put the job
breakdown into a table:*

#	Activity	Preceding activity	Duration (Seconds)
	Start	N/A	N/A
A	Fill kettle	A	25
B	Plug in kettle	B	5
C	Turn kettle on and boil	C	180
D	Pour milk into mug	START	5
E	Put tea into mug	D	5
F	Put sugar into mug	E	5
G	Pour boiling water into mug	C and F	10
H	Stir	G	5
	End	H	N/A

The next step is to draw the network based upon the
information in the job breakdown. There are a few rules to
consider here.

1 A node – a circle, represents each activity.

2 Each node holds three pieces of information – a node number (10, 20, 30 etc), an *earliest event time* (the earliest point at which the activity can start), and a *latest event time* (the latest possible time all activities arriving at an event can finish without delaying the project).

3 Events are linked via arrows.

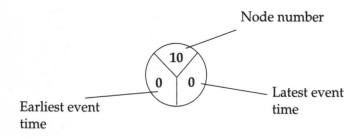

Node number

Earliest event time

Latest event time

The network for making a cup of tea is as follows:

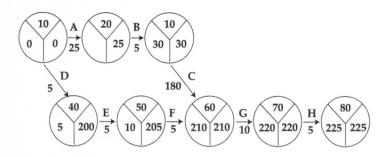

From this Critical Path Analysis we can see it takes a total of 225 seconds to make a cup of tea, provided there is no slippage (or spills!) in the task durations. This time comes about through adding up activity durations through the Critical Path – A, B, C, G, and H. The other activities run *in*

parallel to these and are less crucial to the overall running of the project.

The timings shown in the nodes are calculated through the following method:

First a *forward pass* is run:

- **Forward pass** – this is the process of calculating the earliest time a project can finish. Beginning with the first event – *zero* – the *earliest start time* of each activity is added to its duration. This provides us with the *earliest finish time*. When a single activity arrives at a node (an event), this is taken as the *earliest start time* for that event. When more than one activity arrives at a node, the last of the *earliest finish times* is used. This is because all activities arriving at the node must be complete before any activities leaving it can begin. Once complete, the *forward pass* indicates the earliest completion time for the entire project.

The information calculated during the *forward pass* is then used to calculate the *backward pass:*

- **Backward pass** – this shows the latest time the activities arriving at a node (an event) can finish without delaying the project. The *backward pass* starts at the last event in the network, and deducts each activity's time away from the *latest finishing time*. This gives us the latest time the project can start. When only one activity leaves a node, this is the latest *event time* for that particular event. If there is more than one activity, the earliest of the *latest* *start times* is used. If any other *latest start time were* used, the project would be late in completion.

Project and Operations Management

Having worked through the basics of project management, we need to reconcile it to Operations Management. Some people would argue that such a reconciliation cannot be achieved. What they fail to understand is that project management tools offer the means of implementing new or one-off scenarios with minimal disruption. For example, an organisation moving offices will want to complete the task as quickly as possible. By breaking the office move down into component tasks and using CPA, delays can be minimised. This is one of a multitude of examples CPA can be put to good use for.

Summary

Today we have looked at project management, its nature, features and techniques that in specific circumstances can be used to control inputs being turned into outputs. In so doing we have considered:

- The features of projects
- The project environment
- The five stages of project management
- The four areas of project planning
- Critical Path Analysis

Managing people

Over the last four days we have considered a number of
Operations Management concepts. Each one creates powerful
opportunities if embraced by management and the workforce
together. This however may be the biggest challenge facing
all managers – ensuring the workforce are motivated and
willing to embrace change as and when it is necessary.

Thursday – turn of events

- Managing people
- Leadership and change
- Dealing with change
- Motivation
- Managing change and motivation
- Body language and the psychology of selling

Managing people

It is easy to let the technical side of issues like JIT and TQM
cloud the horizon and take us away from our ultimate vision.
Not having such systems in place can be used as an excuse
for failure. To some degree such points hold some validity –
after all, they were devised to make improvements so any
organisation not using them may well be missing out on their
potential benefits. However, what we tend to overlook is that
it is the workforce that makes an organisation succeed – the
technical tools can only assist here.

Before any Operations Management concepts are introduced,
it is important for managers to think carefully about

themselves and how they deal with the workforce. If their dealings generally end in confrontation, the costs of this are incalculable – consider how much time is wasted while the individual in question tells everyone about how badly he or she has been treated. Then add up all the time everyone else wastes thinking it through and working out a defence strategy should the same thing happen to them!

It is therefore important for the Operations Manager to consider how people perceive them. Is it the way you want to be thought of or not? This is a very difficult point to deliberate over, but is important none-the-less. It is possibly easier to deal with if, when you have just finished talking to someone you ask yourself the question 'how would I feel about the way I was just treated if I was that person'.

ALL I ASKED HIM TO DO WAS CHANGE THE WAY WE WORK TO MAKE IT A BIT MORE INTERESTING FOR STAFF...

If your response is negative, then it's time to make changes! Remember that very often, people respond to the ways they are treated rather than to the underlying message. There is no point in having the *"well, it wouldn't bother me if I was spoken to like that, Fred"* attitude when *Fred* is upset. The point is it bothered *Fred* and that is all there is to it! Managing people is all about managing perceptions. Remember, words are powerful: used incorrectly, they can have disastrous results.

Leadership and change

One of the problems we face when making changes comes from individuals' past experiences. In the 1980s and 1990s, people were inundated with continuous waves of change, each promising to deliver what the previous ones had failed to do. The promises eventually grew thin, making people cynical and sceptical when new changes were introduced.

It is therefore generally accepted that *people* do not like change. There are obviously exceptions, as some people are drawn to careers that embrace it, but those of us who do *not* like change tend to resist it whenever possible – we put barriers in the way hoping to prevent or slow down the inevitable. It is worth bearing in mind that most changes in themselves are trivial. Individuals may, however, *perceive* a change differently and consequently build it up into something else. As a result, the *real* task managers face is to deal with peoples' emotions towards change rather than the change itself.

As managers therefore, if we are to implement change and motivate colleagues we must also be *leaders*. In his book, *A Force for Change*, John Kotter (Professor of Organisational Behaviour at Harvard Business School) promotes the issue that leadership promotes change – he emphasises that the main purpose of leadership is to change both *how* and *what* is done through three pivotal functions:

- Establishing direction
- Aligning people
- Motivating and inspiring

Through these functions, Kotter sees the leader as someone who enables and facilitates others, thriving on the achievements of oneself and others.

John Adair (Professor of Leadership Studies at the University of Surrey) in his books *Action-Centred Leadership and Understanding Motivation* promotes three matters managers ought to consider at the same time:

- Task needs
- Individual needs
- Team needs

He goes on to define the main functions leaders need to carry out to meet these needs as:

- Planning
- Informing
- Initiating
- Supporting
- Controlling
- Evaluating

So far we have considered change as a problem. It is worth noting that change is not always *negative* - it can ultimately bring with it very positive effects. A recent case highlights this point brilliantly:

The legal department in a medium sized organisation had been located in particularly poor accommodation. Paint was peeling off the walls, windows leaked and rattled in the wind. The final blow came when an upstairs toilet flushed all over one member of staff whose desk was situated below it!
Brand new premises were found and decorated accordingly. New office furniture and equipment was installed and management expected everyone to be delighted with the new, clean environment.

When the employees finally moved into their new accommodation they appreciated the improvements in the new facilities, but many of them felt uncomfortable in the new surroundings. The bottom line was they did not like the change. The new office, for all its benefits and luxury was still a change they had to grow accustomed to.

But within a few weeks, not only had the team grown accustomed to the new office environment, their output had increased substantially – the change worked!

Change and attitude

Attitude is determined largely by our own minds – in fact 90% of it, with only 10% being determined by the outside world. Managing change therefore forces us to manage attitude. A quote from Carnegie sums this up:

> "Two men looked out through prison bars. One saw mud, the other the stars"

In order to manage change, we must accept that:

- Change affects all aspects of life
- Change is inevitable
- Change is not necessarily quick
- No amount of change can achieve the perfect solution
- Resistance to change is not always a bad thing
- Change requires planning and control
- Changes are only successful when everyone involved is kept informed

Motivation

If we want to make changes we need to motivate people – the individuals that make the changes a reality at the end of the day.

When motivating people, remember that:

- Motivation is personal to the individual – nobody can motivate anyone else
- There is no guaranteed method of motivation
- People are motivated by different things
- Fear cannot motivate people
- Truly motivated individuals are positive, gracious and hold self worth – for themselves and others!
- We can develop motivation in ourselves and others through encouragement

On Monday, we looked at a chronology of management theorists. Some – F. W. Taylor being the first – were keen advocates of treating employees as money motivated machines. Others argued that employees were all individuals and needed more subtle forms of motivation to get the best from them (Herzberg even argued that money came only fifth out of a list of ten factors linked to motivation).

No matter which view one takes, certain human traits exist – particularly when we deal with people at work. Consider for example a baby learning to walk. At first it keeps falling down. What do the adults around it do? Tell it off for not walking correctly in the first place? Of course not – they pick the baby up and encourage it to try again – they jump around and clap enthusiastically so the baby knows when it is doing the right thing. Similar situations occur throughout a child's life in different situations until the day he or she goes to work for the first time. On this day tasks are assigned, but the first time a mistake is made, the individual is reprimanded and told to get it right in future. We expect this to have a positive effect on the individual's performance and are surprised when the subject becomes withdrawn and reticent to try again.

Why do we apply one theory of motivation to a baby and child, yet a different one to an adult that is inexperienced? Surely lack of experience is a common thread? If we were to motivate adults using positive means of reinforcement, would the end results not be improved? Would this not reduce waste, and ultimately improve the organisation's financial position? If we believe it would, it is vitally important for organisations to embrace motivation as a major tool in the competition stakes.

Body Language and the psychology of selling

As an Operations Manager it is vitally important to be aware of how we appear to others – how we dress, stand, what habits we have, our use of words and body language. Once we understand how we appear to others, we become aware of what other people are *really* telling us. It gives us the tools to positively read invisible and often-subconscious signals transmitted to us by individuals during our dealings with them.

It is a surprising fact that 90% or more of all human communication takes place through non-verbal means. It is therefore vitally important to ensure that Operations Managers can read and understand these signals as they happen. Accordingly, an important aspect of dealing with people is having the ability to read and use body language and psychology effectively. Obviously, some people are more gifted than others when dealing with people – they adjust their body language and posture according to the situation – and they are totally unaware that they do it. The rest of us have to learn how to take control of the situation.

We can learn a lot from *salespeople* here. To make a sale and provide the customer with what is required, they try to make customers *open up* and provide as much information as possible.

When dealing with a customer regarding a trade-in, a tried and tested car sales technique is to open the bonnet of the vehicle and compliment its cleanliness and the care the owner has lavished on it. This happens even if it is covered in oil and dirt and has never been serviced! The customer is generally flattered and details every little problem the car has ever had.

Should the salesperson open the bonnet and say: "what a mess – when did you last have this serviced?" the customer would hardly be impressed, and would try to hide as much as possible until the deal was struck.

It was Abraham Lincoln who said:

"If you would win a man to your cause, first convince him that you are his sincere friend."

For an Operations Manager this implies that to have someone fulfil a task for you, you have to sell yourself first and make sure you are liked. The Operations Manager is therefore a salesperson in disguise, selling himself or herself first, and concepts, ideas and methods of working second. If people accept the *sale* then the work will be done as required, the only difference being that the Operations Manager is selling to colleagues who will not walk away with a product or service at the end of the deal. It may be beneficial for an Operations Manager to learn more about the art of selling to become increasingly effective.

We are not expected to become sales professionals here, but aware of common sales techniques. For example, sales professionals often subtly mimic buyers as a form of subconscious flattery to make a sale. They alter the tone and strength of voice, posture, rate of breathing and even the clothes they wear. They also become aware of the different body signals customers display.

Therefore when dealing with individuals and groups, remember the following:

- Keep eye contact with your audience
- Use individual's names to keep their attention and personalise the situation
- Make the subject feel comfortable
- Be conscious of hand gestures and tone of voice
- Repeat important phrases to strengthen your message
- Use drawings and diagrams to strengthen your message if necessary
- Sound enthusiastic
- Take natural pauses and breaks
- Read other peoples' body language
- Don't be distracted by others
- Ask for other peoples' opinions
- Remain sincere and calm
- Look professional

MY BOSS TOLD ME TO WORK ON MY BODY LANGUAGE

Those in the world of NLP or Neuro-Linguistic Programming suggest we *think* in terms of our senses. So when dealing with an individual, it is possible to tailor our form of communication to their *thinking* strength.

The key senses are:

- **Visual** – *thinking* in picture form
- **Auditory** – *thinking* in sound form
- **Kinesthetic** – *thinking* in feeling form
- **Olfactory** – *thinking* in terms of smell
- **Gustatory** – *thinking* in terms of taste

So how do we know how people *think*? If you are in the middle of a conversation with someone who says *"that sounds to me like . . ."* you have a good idea he or she is thinking in an auditory sense. If on the other hand the reply is *"I see what you are saying"* then all indications point to the visual sense. If we know that someone is a *visual thinker*, we can tailor a conversation to their needs by drawing diagrams or introducing pictures, plans or maps to help illustrate a point. Not only will this help us make our point more clearly, it will also make the other person feel as though we have taken the time and trouble to work to their strengths – thus motivating them!

A word to the wise here – whilst reading body language is important, it is more important to ensure we deal with the true issue at hand. There is no point in concentrating solely on body language signs to discover we have missed the point at the end of the conversation.

Summary

We have spent Thursday considering how we deal with, lead and motivate people. We have incorporated:

- The powerful use of words when managing individuals
- The links between Leadership and Change, and how two gurus see them working together
- Motivation issues from some of the earliest to the present day
- The importance of body language and NLP in management

Operations Management and computers

Today we turn our attention to computers and their influences on Operations Management. The effect computers have had on industry is monumental – not only from an *output* point of view, but also from a *personnel* perspective.

Friday – turn of events

- Operations Management and IT
- Computer Aided Design (CAD)
- Computer Aided Manufacture (CAM)
- Computer Integrated Manufacture (CIM)
- Electronic Data Interchange (EDI)
- Simulation
- Decision Support Systems (DSS)
- Executive Information Systems (EIS)

Operations Management and IT

Many people ask what interest Operations Managers have in Information Technology – after all, computers have traditionally had no place on the *shop floor*.

The common belief that Information Technology and computers are one and the same thing is not strictly true. Information Technology is concerned with the free flow of information in an organisation, whether this is through paper or technologically based means. Computers happen to be put to widespread use in IT systems because of their speed, accuracy and efficiency.

As today's Operations Manager has such a wide area of responsibility, any tool that can ease the task ought to be welcomed.

An IT system should integrate the following for an Operations Manager:

- Work schedules
- Inventory / stock control
- Personnel
- Product and service design
- Planning, scheduling and control
- Vendor selection
- Costs, e.g. shipping
- MRP, MRPII, JIT, OPT etc.

COME ON THEN EINSTEIN, WHAT'S THIS COMPUTER THING GOOD FOR THEN?

Computer Aided Design – CAD

Traditionally, skilled personnel using pen and paper have drafted plans. Computers revolutionised the process, allowing designs to be created and adjusted as often as required on a screen, then printed later.

In the early days of computer use, CAD design packages were quite inflexible. Since then, their advancement has been meteoric, to the point where specialist CAD packages are commonly used on home PCs for different tasks. A quantity surveyor for example can now map out a site, provide geographic details and stipulate the work to be done (such as the required depth of a hole) and the CAD software will calculate how much earth will be moved – and give an estimate of how long it will take to do the job.

The benefits of such a system are:

- Increased flexibility
- Increased output
- Faster job turnaround
- Changes are easier to make
- Past work can be saved and adapted for new jobs

Numerically controlled machines

In the 1950s, an American company created a process for controlling machines that made helicopter blades. All instructions were stored on paper tape and fed into the machines as x, y, *and* z coordinates – the Numerically Controlled machine was born. The only difference between NC machines then and now is that modern NC machines

make use of their own computer rather than paper tape.
Contrary to popular belief, NC machines are relatively easy
to operate – once a training programme has been completed.
Their great benefit is the ability to manufacture the same
components continuously without breaks or human
intervention.

Computer Aided Design/Computer Aided Manufacture – CAD/CAM

Once a component has been designed using CAD equipment,
it is possible to load the design information into an NC
machine and have the machine control the production side of
the process. This is CAD/CAM.

Computer Integrated Manufacture – CIM

CAD and CAM show their greatest benefits when integrated together. However, it is possible to push the boundaries one step further by integrating the delivery of materials to the machines as and when needed from the storeroom. In a perfect world, there is not even a need for human interaction as the machines do it all!

Electronic Data Interchange – EDI

Whilst all these computer-related Operations Management tools seem effective, some people will have noticed that they are dedicated to a manufacturing environment. Can they be utilised in the service sector?

The answer is of course yes, but the context of their use must be considered carefully:

In UK supermarkets computers are used to show stock levels on the shelves and warehouse inventory, as well as human resource requirements and available personnel. Some Japanese supermarkets have taken the IT concept one step further.

They make use of a central store computer that tracks all stocks of goods on the shelves. When an item is sold, its barcode is scanned through the checkout and the computer acknowledges this by reducing its inventory level by one.

At the end of each working day, the computer calculates the total sales, subtracts that figure from the original number of items on display at the start of the day and places orders for more. The most exciting aspect of this system is that the computer, knowing the number of products sold, instructs robots to re-stack the shelves.

Computer simulation

Computer simulations are mathematical models of real life situations that allow the user to alter features and see the results that would occur.

Most computer simulation models are applied to situations that cannot easily or safely be applied to real life. One example is the simulation of a nuclear blast that incorporates heat, velocity and radioactive emissions. It is safer, less costly and destructive to simulate such a test rather than try it out for real! Not all business simulations are as explosive, and simple models can be constructed on a spreadsheet.

Simulation can help an organisation to:

- Create new knowledge
- Reduce re-learning
- Understand the impact of business changes
- Understand the impact of strategic changes
- Solve problems
- Encourage and facilitate learning/training

Decision Support Systems – DSS

Decision Support Systems are similar to computer simulation in as much as they allow the user to develop computer *what if* scenarios. They are intended to *support* managers when making decisions – they do not *make* the decision. Decision Support Systems are most effective when:

- There is a large database of background information
- Large volumes of data require computer processing
- There are complex relationships among the data
- A number of people are involved in tackling a problem with their own areas of expertise when the computer works as a coordinator
- There is staged analysis of the problem
- A human decision is required from a range of solutions

Executive Information Systems – EIS

An EIS delivers a summary from a wide area of information, generally to senior managers, thus allowing them to make and plan for strategic decisions.

Operations Management and computers in service industries

Many individuals argue that the computer systems mentioned so far are still only useful in manufacturing environments and service organisations have no use for them. To a degree this is true.

It is, however, worth bearing in mind the fact that these technologies are still in their infancy, and are not yet universally used throughout all industry.

Judging from some of the reactions they received in the 1940s and 1950s, computers have come a long way:

- "I think there's a world market for maybe five computers." (Thomas Watson, 1943, Chairman of IBM)
- "Computers in the future will weigh no more than 1.5 tons." (From Popular Mechanics, 1949)
- "I have travelled the length and breadth of this country and talked to the best people, and I can assure you that data processing is a fad that won't last out the year." (The editor in charge of business books at Prentice-Hall Publishers, 1957)

If we look back throughout history, each time new technology has been introduced it has initially had only one specific intended use. Over time it has been adapted for other applications. As computers and their programmes were designed initially for scientific and military purposes, who would have thought that over a few short decades they would be incorporated into appliances in every home in the country? Who would have considered that computers would replace the typist?

From this line of argument, it is fair to assume that technology, such as CAD/CAM, could well be integrated into the service sector in some form in years to come.

AND I KNOW YOU WILL BELIEVE ME WHEN I SAY THAT THIS THEORY WILL BE USED IN THE SERVICE SECTOR IN THE FUTURE

For the time being though, we can see the following uses for computer technology in Operations Management:

Technological tool	Service organisation use
CAD	Quantity surveying
CIM	Internet book shop/catalogue showroom
EDI	Supermarkets, data processing departments, D.S.S.

Simulation	H.M. Treasury – Economic Forecasts. Met Office – Weather forecasts
DSS	Charities making spending decisions when concerned about the economic outlook
EIS	Executives working on an organisational strategy

Summary

We have spent today looking at how computers and computer systems can help us manage operations. In so doing we have looked at:

- An overview of information technology
- An overview of computer controlled machines
- The integration of computers and technology to assist both service and manufacturing organisations in the tasks they face
- The use of computers in assisting managers whilst making decisions

The strategic challenge facing Operations Management

Before summarising Operations Management, we will today consider the long-term issues facing Operations Managers – organisation strategies and the possibility of hybrid solutions.

Saturday – turn of events

- Time management
- Mission statement and strategy
- The strategic challenge facing Operations Management
- Hybrid concepts
- Summary

Time management

One of the problems facing Operations Managers is lack of time – there are too few hours in the day to ensure all tasks are complete. Whilst few would argue with this sentiment, truly successful people in *every* walk of life take care of time – they do not let it rule them.

We don't have the space to consider *time management* in detail here, but when one is *pushed for time* it is worth considering whether the task in hand is *urgent* or *important* – there is a big difference! *Urgent* tasks are those that cannot be put off – not completing them will lose business and possibly jobs. *Important* tasks are slightly different – every task ought at least to be important. If a job is not important, then why bother with it – it's a waste of time, effort and money?

Operations Managers have particular stresses put on their time – they are juggling practically every aspect of the business on a daily basis. They must therefore accept that there will never be time for everything. The trick to time management is to focus on the steps that lead to the goal.

Thus:

> 15 minutes of concentrated application can produce greater results than fifteen hours of diluted effort

The mission statement

An organisation's mission statement is a document stating its business intent. It is written for the benefit of all employees so that they are aware of the fundamental codes and goals the organisation operates to. An effective mission statement is a powerful tool as it directs and motivates employees, empowering them in their jobs and driving the organisation forward. We have already mentioned that *words* are powerful. A badly expressed mission statement is at best useless and at worst, the victim of employee ridicule. It is therefore in the best interest of every Operations Manager and organisation to have a well-written mission statement.

Strategy

The strategic concept originates form the Greek word *strategia* meaning "leadership". A strategy is a plan dedicated to achieving an organisation's long-term aims and objectives. Consequently, it is not cast in stone, and must be constantly changed and rewritten according to the competition and market trends.

Whilst strategies must be reviewed constantly, there have been strategic trends in the last three decades that organisations have tended to follow.

These are:

- In the 1970s, organisational strategy centered on market attractiveness – organisations were interested in acquiring a strategic portfolio of products and services that were offered for sale
- Throughout the 1980s, organisation strategy focused on organisation strength – profit in itself was not seen as the main focal point. Three basic courses of action suggested generic strategies – overall cost leadership, product differentiation and focus
- During the 1990s, the quality concept was integrated into organisation strategic plans; TQM was widely adopted and seen to be the only way to survive in the future

It is the role of senior management to develop an organisation's strategy, taking all internal and external factors into account.

Their strategic concerns include:

- Deciding what is best for the organisation
- Deciding what is best for the working situation
- Deciding what is best for the employees
- Including all those individuals involved
- Deciding upon top down or bottom up management

Only by understanding the organisational mission statement *and* strategy can the Operations Manager effectively employ any tools dealt with this week in an appropriate manner.

There are of course individuals who will always ask *"what if we get it wrong?"* Whenever any decision has to be made there is a possibility that it can be wrong. The only people who never make mistakes are those that never do anything. Operations Management is about making decisions – sometimes tough ones in the face of adversity – and working through to a final result. This of course does not guarantee a good outcome, but it does guarantee an outcome, nonetheless. What should we do if an outcome isn't the one expected? Perhaps change the inputs; alter the process, the system or behaviour until we get the outputs we want!

The strategic challenge facing Operations Management

We are at the dawn of a new millennium. The opportunities that lie before us are unprecedented. Global competition is most definitely part of our lives, and computerisation has changed the way we live forever. We are forced to work faster and harder than at any time before to "out-psyche" our competitors and win orders.

The introduction to this book tells the parable of the *Titanic Management Principle*. Whilst its words are frank, they are realistic and based around real experiences; many of us spend our working lives *fire-fighting* rather than fulfilling the job we are paid to do. We fall into the *Titanic Management* trap because we are too busy to see the *iceberg* approaching.

Operations Managers hold the key to the future of organisations, and to survive, organisational strategy must incorporate **Operations Management** principles and practice. By remaining *customer* and not *product* oriented, organisations can maintain their market position and avoid the *Titanic Management* fate. All industries exist because they are there to satisfy cutomer needs – they are not there because they can simply produce goods or services. Organisations failing to adapt to market trends are likely to have lost sight of their need to satisfy customers. Their market position and power is never taken away by a competitor – it is given away by themselves.

The Strategic Challenge facing Operations Management therefore requires the *operations* side of the organisation to become its central hub, ensuring products and services are second to none. At the same time organisations must be sure their external links with customers are strong enough to obtain specific, measurable, accurate, relevant and timely feedback that can be used in the future to make improvements and ensure that customers remain loyal.

Hybrid concepts

We have discussed numerous Operations Management concepts and the question will no doubt be asked as to which one to choose. This is a difficult question to answer without knowing all relevant facts. It is also down to the judgement and experience of the Operations Manager. Practically speaking, the answer is likely to be found in a *hybrid* solution.

Rather than taking an Operations Management philosophy

and implementing it in its totality into an organisation, the world now requires a more realistic approach. Throughout the last six days we have looked at a number of Operations Management concepts. Some of them will no doubt contain useful points you feel could benefit your organisation – others do not. A hybrid concept takes the useful elements of different Operations Management philosophies and mixes them into a unique recipe that works *for you or your organisation*. It need never work for anyone else, and is unlikely to be illustrated in a book – but if it works for you then it works! Customers are not generally interested in how we complete their orders – as long as we *do* complete them, and match their requirements at the same time.

Therefore experiment and don't follow the crowd! Have the people working with you, who know and understand the job from its grass roots put their views forward. If they get it wrong then move on from that as a learning experience.

Always remember:

> An organisation not progressing is standing still
>
> An organisation standing still today will flounder tomorrow

Summary

On the last day of our week, we have considered the long-term issues facing Operations Managers. We have thought through:

- How effective time management can assist the Operations Manager
- The use and abuse of mission statements in organisations
- What strategy is and the strategic challenge organisations face
- What *hybrid* concepts are and why organisations should adopt their own

During this week we have covered Operations Management methods, principles and concepts that can bring about powerful and immediate results. The topics covered can be summarised as:

Overview of Operations Management (Sunday)

- Operations Management heritage

- Reasons for studying Operations Management

- Understanding customers

- Introduction to quality

Output Concepts (Monday)

The control of outputs through a number of different Operations Management philosophies:

- The Just in Time (JIT) principle

- The Just in Case (JIC) principle

- The importance of layout to Operations Managers
- Material Requirements Planning (MRP)
- Manufacturing Resource Planning (MRP II)

Quality (Tuesday)

An overview of the different kinds of quality ethos used throughout the last century:

- TQM
- BPR
- British and International Standards
- SPC
- Quality Awards

Project planning (Wednesday)

A brief analysis of the nature and tools of projects, and their uses to the Operations Manager:

- Project planning and control
- Critical Path Analysis

Managing people (Thursday)

As Operations Management is not simply about systems and machines, it is vitally important to consider how we manage and deal with people:

- Leadership

- Change

- Motivation

- Body language

Operations Management and Computers (Friday)

The importance and relevance of computers to Operations Managers in both the service and manufacturing sectors:

- CAD (Computer Aided Design)

- CAM (Computer Aided Manufacture)

- CIM (Computer Integrated Manufacture)

- EDI (Electronic Data Interchange)

- Simulation

- DSS (Decision Support Systems)

- EIS (Executive Information Systems)

The strategic challenge facing Operations Management (Saturday)

The links between Operations Management and an organisation's strategy have become closely linked. Operations Managers consider more issues than ever before:

- Time management

- Organisation mission statements and strategy
- The *Titanic Management Principle*
- Hybrid concepts

We hope this book has been helpful as an introduction and overview of Operations Management. To enquire about Operations Management training, consultancy, and motivational talks with Sean Naughton, contact him via email on:

Email: *Opsmgt@Tesco.net*

NOTES

NOTES

N O T E S

For information

on other

IN A WEEK titles

go to

www.inaweek.co.uk